THE ENDANGERED MAD

Edited by
Albert B. Feldstein

GW00725502

WARNER BOOKS

A Time Warner Company

£1
12/11

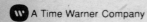

KING KORN

ARTIST: HARRY NORTH, ESQ.
WRITER: DICK DE BARTOLO

KONG-PHEW DEPT.

Well, that old loveable ape is back in the movies. We're referring, of course, to Dino De Laurentiis. Clever Dino has taken the old classic, "King Kong," and he's up-dated it . . . he's put it on the wide screen in color . . . he's invented new special effects . . . and he's added something new: Humor! Yessir, it seems they decided to play this remake for laughs! Unfortunately, they don't go far enough! Because all they end up with is

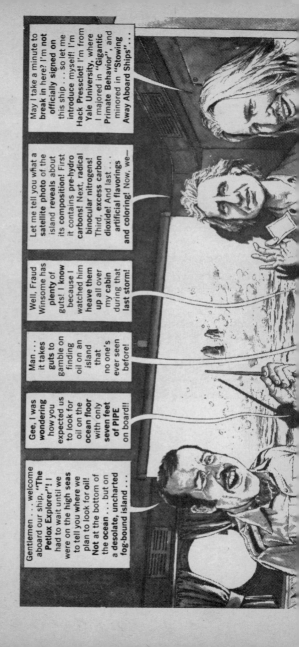

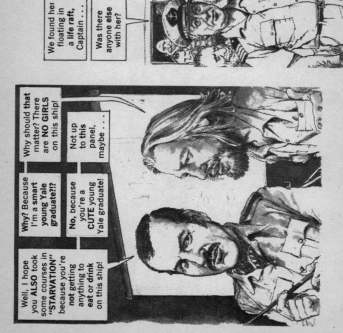

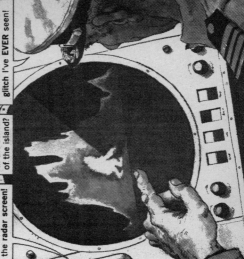

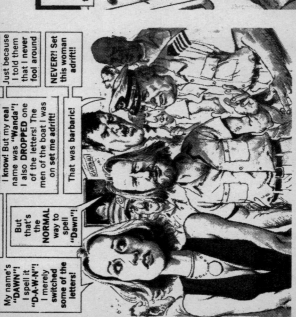

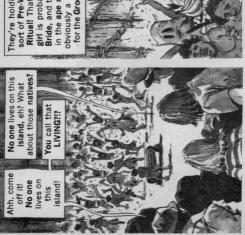

Ahh, come off it! No one lives on this island!

No one lives on this island, eh? What about those natives?

You call that LIVING?!?

They're holding some sort of **Pre-Wedding Ritual**! That native girl is probably the **Bride**, and that guy in the ape mask is obviously a stand-in for the **Groom** . . .

Because it's **BAD LUCK** for the Bride to see the **REAL Groom** before the Wedding?

Not exactly! In this case, it may be even **WORSE** luck for the Bride when she sees the Groom **AFTER** the Wedding!!

Baggy! Look down there! See those bubbling pools of thick black **gook?** Do you think that could be oil?

I doubt it! The natives are pouring it into cups and adding cream and sugar . . .!

We're too late! King has already taken Dawn...!

Any ideas where?

Well, there's a small candle-lit restaurant overlooking the lagoon next to a motel! That would be my best guess!

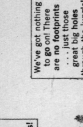

We've got nothing to go on! There are no footprints ...just those great big holes through the jungle!

Those aren't HOLES, you idiot! Those ARE the footprints! C'mon ...

Y'know, King... as big as your hands are, I've had less trouble with you than with most of the men I've dated!

You're not a bad ape! First, you gave me a bath in a jungle pool, then you blew me dry, and now you've brought me a couple of eggs for breakfast ...

Er... you wouldn't happen to have a twelve-foot frying pan, would you?!?

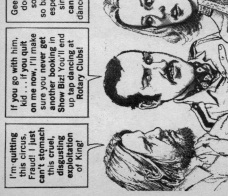

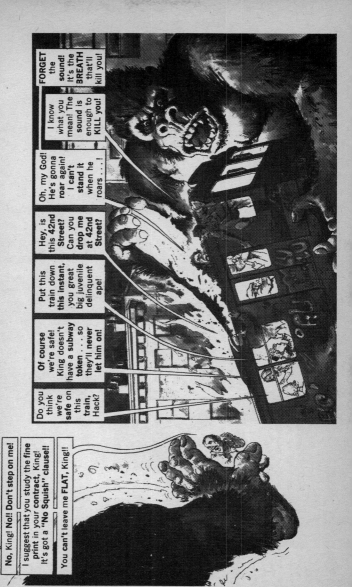

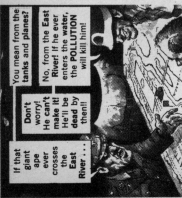

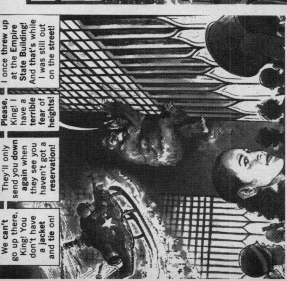

ONE NIGHT ON SKULL ISLAND

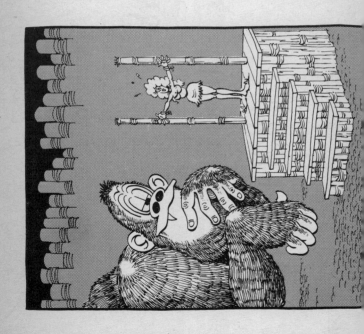

A MAD PEEK
BEHIND THE SCENES

CAR RENTAL
COMPANIES

ARTIST: BOB CLARKE
WRITER: STAN HART

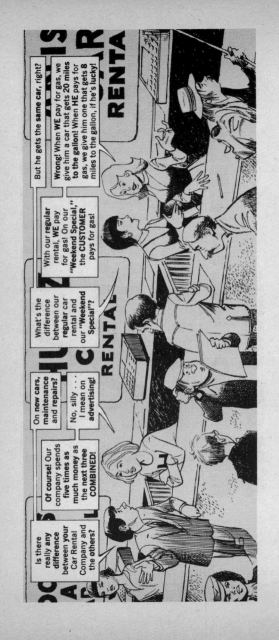

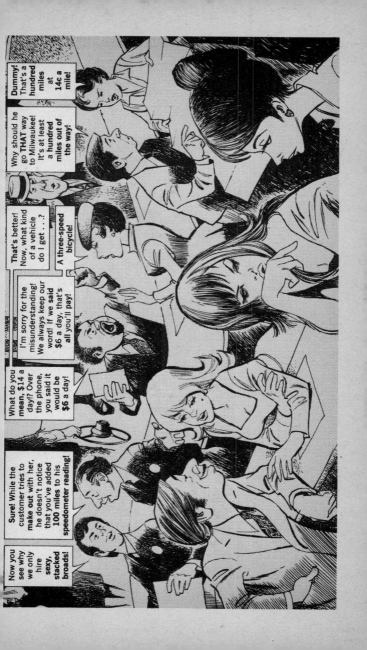

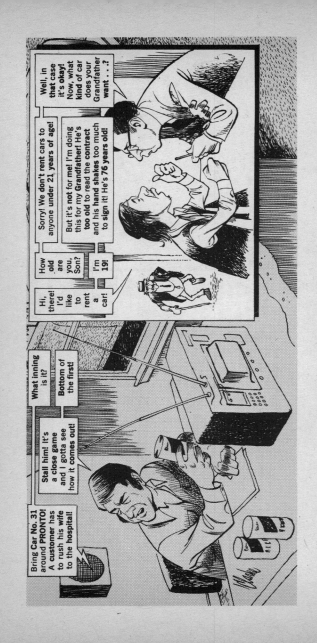

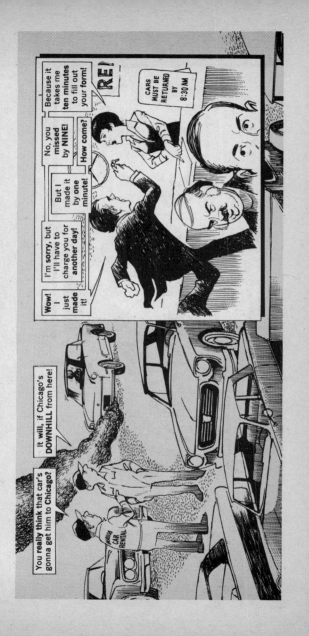

THE LIGHTER SIDE OF...

CONS

Darn it! The **television set** is broken! Now, it's gonna cost me an **arm** and a leg to get it **fixed!**

Jack's TV Repair always **overcharges** me! I know I'm gonna be **taken!**

So don' call Jack'

MMERS

WRITER & ARTIST:
DAVID BERG

Stop by the **Supermarket** on the way home . . .

Oh, NO!! You know how I hate shopping!

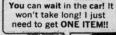

You can wait in the car! It won't take long! I just need to get **ONE ITEM!!**

FIVE BAGS?!? I thought you said you only needed to get **ONE ITEM . . . ?!?**

I did . . .

FOOD!!

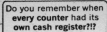

ONE
TUESDAY
MORNING
ON
MAIN STREET

What's going on in Nursery Land these days? Well, Tom, Tom the Piper's Son is stuffing ballot boxes, and Jack and Mrs. Sprat are splitting their votes between the Democrats and G.O.P. In other words, it's voting time for Solomon Grundy and his friends, which is our way of introducing . . .

MAD'S

ELECTION-YEAR

MOTHER GOOSE

ARTIST: PAUL COKER, JR.   WRITER: FRANK JACOBS

Humpty Dumpty

Humpty Dumpty made an address;
Humpty Dumpty hollered, "Spend less!"
All the conservative voters agreed
That Humpty in office was sure to succeed.

Humpty Dumpty spoke to the poor;
Humpty Dumpty hollered, "Spend more!"
All of the liberal voters concurred
That Humpty by far was the one they preferred.

Humpty Dumpty stays on the fence;
Humpty Dumpty knows this makes sense;
He'll win all the voters up North and down South
By making full use of both sides of his mouth.

Little Bo Peep

Little Bo Peep
Is fast sleep
And that's the way she'll stay;
Little Jack Horner
Lies flat in his corner
And won't wake up today;
Little Boy Blue
Is dozing, too—
There isn't a soul who's awake;
Why are they snoring?
From hearing those boring
Long speeches their candidates make.

Sing a Song of Issues

Sing a song of issues,
Of unemployment rates,
Of busing and of housing,
Of greater aid to states;
When the campaign's over,
We can guarantee
We'll make the man the winner
Who looked best on TV.

The Crooked Man

There was a crooked man,
And he had a crooked laugh,
And he ran a crooked office,
And he hired a crooked staff.

He served a crooked term,
And he did a crooked job,
And he rammed through crooked bills
For a crooked local mob.

Why back the crooked man
When his crooked ways you see?
Because the rival candidate
Is crookeder than he.

Wee Willie Winkie

Wee Willie Winkie
Doesn't seem for real,
Takes no contributions,
Never makes a deal.

Wee Willie Winkie
Always comes off clean,
Free from all corruption,
Owned by no machine.

Wee Willie Winkie
Rids himself of sin;
Maybe that's why Willie
Never seems to win.

Harry is a Congressman

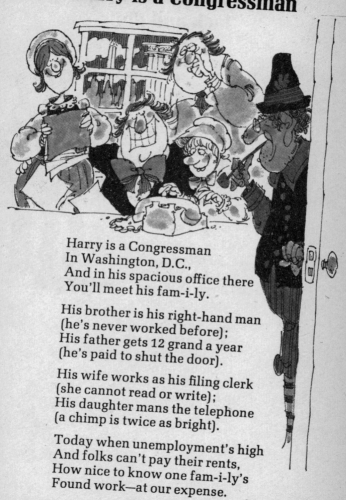

Harry is a Congressman
In Washington, D.C.,
And in his spacious office there
You'll meet his fam-i-ly.

His brother is his right-hand man
(he's never worked before);
His father gets 12 grand a year
(he's paid to shut the door).

His wife works as his filing clerk
(she cannot read or write);
His daughter mans the telephone
(a chimp is twice as bright).

Today when unemployment's high
And folks can't pay their rents,
How nice to know one fam-i-ly's
Found work—at our expense.

Jack and Phil

Jack and Phil
Work on the Hill;
Two Senators are they;
But they pursue
The work they do
In quite a diff'rent way.

Jack's a slob
Who muffs his job,
While Phil achieves perfection;
It should be clear
Which one this year
Is up for re-election.

The Other Day Upon the Stair

The other day upon the stair
I saw a man who wasn't there;
He wasn't there again today;
I think he's from the C.I.A.

Taffy Was a Rich Man

Taffy was a rich man;
Taffy was connected;
Taffy spent five hundred grand
To get his man elected.

Taffy's now Ambassador
And struts around with pride;
Why don't you spend five hundred grand
And you'll be qualified.

As I Was Watching NBC

As I was watching NBC,
I heard a newsman telling me
Although returns were barely in
That A would lose and B would win.

As I was watching CBS,
I heard an analyst profess
That his computer could foresee
That C should now concede to D.

As I was watching ABC,
I heard that F would unseat E,
And, from 12 votes in Tennessee,
That H would wind up beating G.

As I turned off my set, I swore,
"What good are voters anymore?
"We might as well get rid of them
"And leave the vote to IBM."

Tweedledum and Tweedledee

Tweedledum and Tweedledee
Were running for the House,
When Tweedledum smeared Tweedledee
By calling him a louse.

Tweedledee said Tweedledum
Had caused a vicious stink,
Then spread the word that Tweedledum
Was going to a "Shrink."

Tweedledum said Tweedledee
Was vile and full of bunk;
"The problem is," said Tweedledum,
"That Tweedledee's a drunk."

Tweedledee said Tweedledum
Was wrong in ev'ry way,
Then whispered to a columnist
That Tweedledum was gay.

Today I heard that Tweedledee
Was spotted at an orgy;
To hell with both—Election Day
I'll write in Georgie Porgie!

Despite the Crooks Unbeatable

Despite the crooks unbeatable—
Those creepy clods unseatable—
With dirty deals despicable
That make the voters trickable—

Despite folks made insensible
From views incomprehensible
In speeches unendurable
By party hacks incurable—

Despite campaigns regrettable
With promises forgettable—
Despite the rumors spreadable—
Our system works—Incredible!

A favorite Grown-Up complaint is that kids today don't know or care what's going on in the world. Well, what do they expect? A whole generation is being raised on the confusing double-talk of TV News. And maybe Parents can con themselves into thinking they understand all those mysterious new words and

A LITT
GUID
UNDERS
THE N

ARTIST: JACK DAVIS

bewildering new phrases of the TV Newscaster . . . but their kids are too honest to do that. They're the first ones to admit that they need help in deciphering the indecipherable. And so . . . MAD rushes to the aid of the younger generation with this vital Public Service Feature entitled:

LE KID'S
E TO
ANDING
NEWS

WRITER: TOM KOCH

Classified Information

. . . is like the kind your Teacher writes in a note to your Parents, and then seals the envelope so you can't find out what it is, even though you're the one she's written about.

A Nuclear Deterrent

. . . is like when your folks buy a dog just so they can put a "Beware Of The Dog" sign on the front gate to scare away strangers . . . they hope.

Granting Diplomatic Recognition

. . . is like when you invite a kid to your Birthday Party—even though you don't like him very much—because you know he'll bring an expensive present.

Strategic Arms Limitations

. . . is like when two guys agree to throw away so many weapons, they barely have enough left to kill each other more than once.

A Conflict of Interest

. . . is like when you're assigned as the Honorary Hall Monitor to see that nobody snitches stuff out of the lockers, and you're the main one who's snitching stuff.

A Recession

. . . is when your allowance stays the same for a long time because your Father asked for a raise and got turned down.

A Consumer Boycott

. . . is when all the Mothers get together and agree not to buy stuff their kids love to eat until the prices come down. (Oddly enough, Consumer Boycotts are never called to protest the rising costs of Grown-Up things like whiskey, beer and cigarettes.)

A Depression

. . . is when you don't get any allowance at all for a long time because your Father asked for a raise and got fired.

School Desegregation and Forced Busing

. . . are really the same thing. Adults have merely given it two different names so that those who are for it and those who are against it can both make it sound as if the other side is wrong.

A U.N. Cease-Fire

. . . is like when your Mom says it's okay to hit another kid if he hits you first, but not if he just looks like he might.

Bipartisanship

. . . is like when your Mom and Dad are both so completely against letting you take up "Hang Gliding" that there's no point in trying to play one of them off against the other.

An Unannounced Candidate

. . . is like what you are when you see a girl you want to date real bad but you're scared to ask her until her brother can almost guarantee that she won't say "NO!"

Senior Citizens

. . . are what Middle-Aged People call Old People when they want to get rid of them without hurting their feelings.

The Domino Theory

. . . is a Grown-Up term for what happens when your Dad's Boss is forced by his Wife to sleep on the sofa, which makes him yell at your Dad all the next day, which makes your Dad get bombed on his way home from work, which makes your Mom send you upstairs to your room so you won't hear what happens next.

Women's Liberation

. . . is a movement designed to convince everybody that girls with I.Q.s of 160 are as good as boys who can chin themselves 28 times without stopping.

Deficit Spending

. . . is like when you borrow so far ahead on your allowance that you can't ever get out of debt, unless you grow up to be the only 44-year-old person still getting an allowance.

Declaring Bankruptcy

. . . is like when you owe money to all of your friends, and you announce that you're not going to pay it back, but they can't hit you right then because your Father is with you.

A Covert Operation

. . . is what Grown-Ups call it when they get caught doing something they shouldn't do. By calling it that, they make sure of getting a medal instead of going to jail.

Fringe Benefits

. . . are like when you agree to clean out your neighbor's garage for a lousy 50¢ cash because you know there's a whole stack of *Penthouse Magazines* under all that junk.

Detente

. . . is like when the Class Bully agrees to stop threatening to beat you up after you promise to do all his Math homework on your new calculator.

A MAD

AT MOVIE

LOOK MAKING

ARTIST & WRITER: SERGIO ARAGONES

A couple of issues back, we suggested that those "Polish Jokes" you've been breaking up over (. . . that show how stupid Poles are supposed to be!) can't even compare to the "American Jokes" they're telling in Poland (. . . that show how stupid Americans really are!). As a result, MAD has gained many thousands of new fans . . . mainly in Warsaw, Krakow, Lodz and Wladyshawowa! Now, to please all our new-found, intelligent, discerning friends, here are

MORE AMERICAN JOKES

THEY'RE TELLING IN POLAND

ARTIST: PAUL COKER, JR.
WRITER: FRANK JACOBS

What do you call an **American assembly-line worker** who puts the **right-size nut** on the **right-size bolt**?

A skilled worker!

Why must an **American child under 18** attend an **R-rated movie** with an **adult**?

So the kid can **explain what's going on** to him!

Why do Americans take vacations in **messy, crowded campers** full of **screaming kids**?

To get **away** from it all!

What's another term for **American Pornography**?

The **Gross National Product!**

Are you struggling with the problem of what career you should pursue when you grow up (and stop reading this childish trash)? Well there are hundreds of exciting new fields developing all the time! F'rinstance, here's . . .

A MAD LOOK AT SOME EXCITING NEW JOB OPPO

HOUSE PLANT THERAPISTS

House plant fanciers who are finding it difficult to carry on conversations with their beloved plants are hiring our experts to do their talking for them. If you have the gift of gab, not to mention a large amount of Carbon Dioxide in your breath, a well-paid, exciting career awaits you with us.

PROXY PLANT PALAVERS, INCORPORATED
West Babbling Brook, Pennsylvania

RTUNITIES

LOST LUGGAGE TRACERS

Airline companies with bigger planes, plus airline employees with smaller brains mean more and more incidents of lost or strayed luggage, which is resulting in exciting new opportunities for lovers of adventure . . . tracing missing two-suiters and carry-alls into remote areas of the world. If you have the wanderlust, you can cash in on this important new career opportunity. Apply now!

LOST AIRLINE BAGGAGE INSURANCE CORP.
Paris   London   Rome   Rio   Brooklyn

CITY PET TRAINERS

The vociferous objections of non-pet-owners plus the threats of more and more legislation, are making it increasingly difficult for dog and cat lovers to let their little dears make doo on city streets. You can make big money by teaching pets to use bathrooms like everybody else. Successful trainers are in big demand. Earn . . . while you learn our fool-poop method.

APPLY: THE DOGGIE DOO AND DON'T CORP.
1 Oomlop Place   Moundsville, Ga.

Food Label
Information Interpreters

Consumers, confused by today's complicated and tricky food labels are in dire need of assistance. Many Supermarkets are turning to our company, which supplies experts in the highly-skilled art of Food Label Information Interpretation. If you think you can tell whether an 18½ oz. can with a 10-cent credit coupon is a better buy at 87 cents than a 2-pound can at $1.32, we can use you in this exciting new important field.

SUPERMARKET CONSUMER ASSISTANCE CO.
Pennywise St., at Poundfoolish Ave., City

DEEP FREEZE
MORTUARY ATTENDENTS

We have openings for the right people who don't mind working in sub-zero temperatures, serving the increasing number of people who are having their remains stored in the many Deep Freeze Mortuaries springing up around the country. A knowledge of Refrigeration Engineering in case of failure is not a necessity! Your salary paid in cold cash.

Apply: TEMPORAL REST CRYOLIC CRYPTS
Birds' Eye and Swanson Sts., Nome, Alaska

SOCIAL WORKERS FOR
UNEMPLOYED SOCIAL WORKERS

We are looking for experienced Social Workers to help us rehabilitate those Social Workers who have been laid off during the recent city budget cuts. So if you are an unemployed Social Worker, apply now and begin working at counseling other unemployed Social Workers (who, come to think of it, will no longer be unemployed because they'll be doing the same furshlugginer thing!)

DEPARTMENT OF SOCIAL WELFARE
Self-Defeating Section, This City

TODAY'S AIR
QUALITY

✓ FOUL
✓ YECCH
✓ GLITCH
✓ CHOKE
✓ COUGH

UNACCEPTABLE
AIR DETECTORS

If you're seven feet or over, and you can't play basketball, we may be able to use you to help sniff out evidence of air pollution before it gets down to "normal-sized" people in cities around the country. Salaries are high and medical benefits are even higher. Send your height (resumes not necessary) to:

**UNACCEPTABLE
AIR DETECTING CORP.**
Box 235 High Scent, Pennsylvania

MUTILATED
PUNCH-CARD RESTORERS

Ever increasing rates, coupled with ever decreasing quality of service, is causing many irate Utility customers to "fold, spindle or mutilate" the computerized bills we send out. If you have a talent for repairing miniscule objects, we are in dire need of your help. Sharp-eyed experts who can salvage the thousands of abused punchcards returned to us each month are being well-paid. Apply now to:

ABUSED PUNCH-CARD DIVISION OF YOUR LOCAL GAS, ELECTRIC OR TELEPHONE COMPANY

RECALLED CAR DRIVERS

If you think that Evil Kneivel is a sissy compared to yourself, you may be our man! Because there's one kind of driving that's far more dangerous than jumping lined-up busses or picturesque canyons . . . mainly, it's driving late-model cars with faulty steering, brakes, etc., that have been recalled by their manufacturers. Owners of such cars are paying big money to have these death traps driven back to their dealers for the necessary repairs . . . rather than take a chance themselves.

RECALLED CAR CHAUFFEURING SERVICE CO.
"Take The Bus And Leave The Dying To Us!"

WRITE BOX 27, ATTENTION: MR. DEREDEVLE
(Drivers with I.Q.'s over 75 need not apply!)

LATE ONE FRIDAY ON AN UPTOWN STREET CORNER

NIGHT

Several months back (MAD #180 to be exact), we interviewed MAD's "CIA Agent Of The Year," and a lot of people found the article pointed and effective. And so, in the true MAD tradition of zapping those on both sides of an issue, we will proceed to offend those very same people by interviewing...

MAD'S "UNDERGROUND REVOLUTIONARY"

OF THE YEAR

ARTIST: PAUL COKER, JR.
WRITER: LOU SILVERSTONE

The CLODS offered to help 'em, but they said they had ENOUGH trouble ALREADY! You just can't trust those ungrateful Redskins!

What about the conditions of the American Indians! Now, that seems like a worthy cause!

No way! Peace is a real downer! I mean, the war was a scene the kids grooved on! Now it's tough finding a cause to get 'em to riot over!

I suppose the Underground was pleased with the end of the war in Vietnam?

What in the world was that THAT?

That was Regis and Tamara, our former Bomb Experts—and the latest martyrs to the cause of Freedom And Justice To All Peoples!

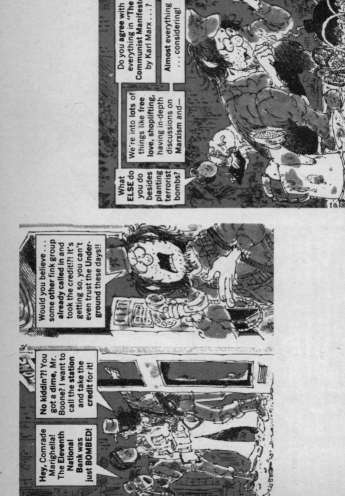

One last question . . . Do you know if there are any FBI or CIA agents in your group?

We **DID** have one Government Undercover fink in the CLODS! Man . . . he was one fantastic Revolutionary! Like, he could always get us bread, or ammo, or electronics, or joints! Too bad we had to kick him out!

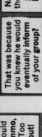

That was because you knew he would eventually inform of your group?

Naah! He had to go because those Government dudes are just too darn VIOLENCE-PRONE . . . even for US!!!

This is Pat Boone . . . signing off and returning you to **MAD** Magazine!

ONE EVENING

AT

A

BANQUET

SALUTING

AN

OUTSTANDING

AMERICAN

Mr. Veeblefetzer, the **National Association of Manufacturers of Inflatables** takes great pleasure in presenting you with this **award** for **"Outstanding Service to the Industry"**...

We have always been intrigued with *The Guiness Book Of World Records*, which lists feats and undertakings that are greater, taller, faster, smaller or older than any others. Recently, MAD began compiling its own set of World Records. And—you know what we found out? We found out that many famous World Records have led to Lesser-Known Follow-Up Records that are even more amazing and stupefying. To show you what we mean, here are excerpts from...

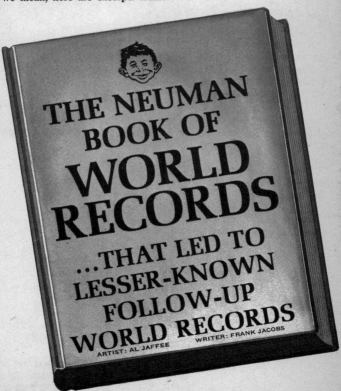

THE NEUMAN
BOOK OF
WORLD
RECORDS
...THAT LED TO
LESSER-KNOWN
FOLLOW-UP
WORLD RECORDS

ARTIST: AL JAFFEE   WRITER: FRANK JACOBS

THE FAMOUS OFFICIAL WORLD RECORD

The World Record for Eating Chocolate Bars was set by Lydia Ann Snavely, of Skroon City, Idaho, who consumed 187 6-ounce Hershey Milk Chocolate Bars in 37 minutes on December 20, 1974.

THE LESSER-KNOWN FOLLOW-UP RECORD

The World Record for Acne was set by Lydia Ann Snavely, of Skroon City, Idaho, who suffered 911 eruptions of facial pimples, hickeys and blemishes between December 20 and 26, 1974.

THE FAMOUS OFFICIAL WORLD RECORD

The Largest Diamond Ever Discovered was found by Mervyn X. Waxbush, who uncovered a stone that weighed 455 carats in a field outside of Pretoria, South Africa, March 13, 1922. The diamond was valued, before cutting, at nearly $5,000,000.

THE LESSER-KNOWN FOLLOW-UP RECORD

The World Record For Marriage Proposals Received By A Man was held by Mervyn X. Waxbush of Pretoria, South Africa, who received 958 proposals of marriage from women between Mar., 1922, and his death from physical exhaustion in August, 1925.

THE FAMOUS OFFICIAL WORLD RECORD

The First Pay Telephone was installed
in New York City on November 1, 1888.

THE LESSER-KNOWN FOLLOW-UP RECORD

**The First Pay Telephone To Go Out Of
order occured in New York City on Nov.
1, 1888, and was reported by Elmo Jay
Finsterhoff. Elmo, incidentally, also
became The First Person To Ever Lose
Money In A Pay Telephone on that date.**

THE FAMOUS OFFICIAL WORLD RECORD

The record for the Fastest Removal Of An Appendix is held by Dr. Ed Greber of Boston, who, working quickly on the morning of June 1, 1955, removed the appendix from a patient in 55 seconds.

THE LESSER-KNOWN FOLLOW-UP RECORD

The record for Most Fingers Accidentally Cut Off During An Operation belongs to Interne Myron Klutz, who had four fingers sliced off while assisting Dr. Ed Greber in Boston on June 1, 1955.

THE FAMOUS OFFICIAL WORLD RECORD

The record for Water Consumption is held by tourist Elmo Yancy, who, on April 10, 1955, drank three gallons in the village of Carramba, Mexico, after he'd crossed the Baja on foot.

THE LESSER-KNOWN FOLLOW-UP RECORD

The record for Kaopectate Consumption is held by Elmo Yancey, who, during a seige of "Montezuma's Revenge," drank the contents of thirty-four 12-ounce bottles from April 10th to 15th, 1966.

The First Golf Course was completed on August 15, 1644 in a field outside the village of Tavish, Scotland, by Angus MacPherson after 7 years of hard work.

The First Golfer To Break A Club In Disgust was Angus MacPherson, after playing three holes of a course near Tavish, Scotland on August 15, 1644.

THE FAMOUS OFFICIAL WORLD RECORD

The World Record for the Greatest Age Difference In A Married Couple was set when Leonard Skaggs, age 112, married Phoebe Weebey, age 16, in a ceremony in Fort Wayne, Indiana, June 3, 1933.

THE LESSER-KNOWN FOLLOW-UP RECORD

The Shortest Honeymoon On Record took place in Fort Wayne, Indiana, June 3, 1933, when Leonard and Phoebe Skaggs checked into the Bridal Suite of the Grand Plaza Hotel at 9:45 P.M., and then checked out 17 minutes later to fly to Reno and file for a divorce.

THE FAMOUS OFFICIAL WORLD RECORD

The Largest Convention in the United States was held May 14th through 19th, 1967, when 14,572 Certified Public Accountants met in the Hilton Hotel in Chicago for their annual meeting.

THE LESSER-KNOWN FOLLOW-UP RECORD

The World Record for Continuous Yawning was held by Wilbur Farquahr, who was a Bellhop in the Hilton Hotel in Chicago, and who yawned without stopping from May 14th to May 18th, 1967.

THE FAMOUS OFFICIAL WORLD RECORD

The Loudest Sound emitted by a mammal is the early Spring mating call of the Spotted Moose of the Northern Yukon, a species that is now near extinction.

THE LESSER-KNOWN FOLLOW-UP RECORD

The Deafest Mammal in the World is the female Spotted Moose of the Northern Yukon, according to scientific tests— which may explain its near extinction.

THE FAMOUS OFFICIAL WORLD RECORD

The First Practical Set of Binoculars was invented in 1657 by Antonio Della Scappini, an Italian scientist, who lived in the crowded city of Gronza.

THE LESSER-KNOWN FOLLOW-UP RECORD

The First Roll-Down Window Shade was invented in 1657 by Rosa Rizzoto, an artists model, for her bedroom window in the crowded Italian city of Gronza.

THE FAMOUS OFFICIAL WORLD RECORD

The Most Ridiculous Magazine Article Ever Published was an idiotic piece called "The Neuman Book Of World Records That Led To Lesser-Known Follow-Up Records! which appeared in issue # 186 of MAD Magazine on Aug. 17, 1976.

THE LESSER-KNOWN FOLLOW-UP RECORD

The Most Subscriptions To A Magazine Ever Cancelled In A Single Day occured the day after issue #186 of MAD Magazine went on sale, Aug. 17, 1976.

ONE DAY
FIVE
THOUSAND
YEARS
AGO

RUMBLE
RUMBLE

THE LIGHTER SIDE OF...

HEALTH NUTS

ARTIST & WRITER:

DAVE BERG

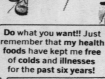

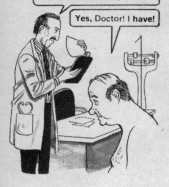

I cannot **believe** that you are actually more than **ONE HUNDRED YEARS OLD!**

I just can't **figure** it! You **break** all the **rules!** You **smoke** like a **chimney!** You **drink hard liquor!** You **eat all the wrong foods!**

Today, we know that **smoking** gives you **cancer,** and that **drinking hard liquor** gives you **cirrhosis** of the **liver,** and that **eating junk foods** is like **eating poison!** So— **how** in heck did you **DO** it?

Maybe because I was **born before they discovered** all those things were **so bad!?!**

David Berg

ONE DAY IN EGYPT

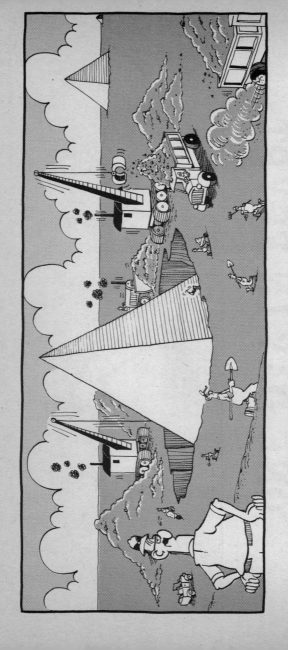

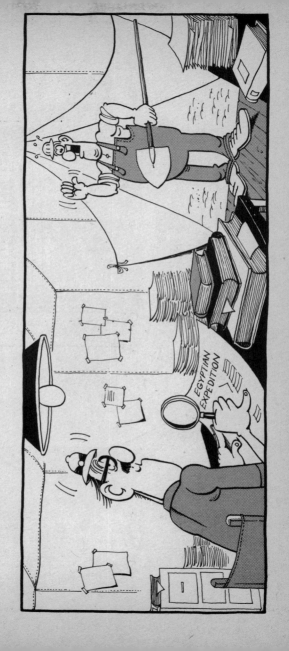

With women making enormous strides toward freedom in recent years, everyone seems to have gotten on the bandwagon, including Television. However, one thing puzzles us: If they must give us all of those "Female-Oriented Situation Comedies," why does TV insist upon making their women characters so damn obnoxious? Take Maude, f'rinstance! Or Rhoda! Or, if you've got an exceptionally strong stomach, Phyllis! And now, the King of the Sit-Coms, Norman Lear, has given us not one, but THREE nauseating females to swallow in one gulp. Namely, a Divorcee and her two daughters. We don't know about you, but we can't digest them all at once. In fact, we can't even take them . . .

ONE DAME AT A TIME

ARTIST: ANGELO TORRES
WRITER: LARRY SIEGEL

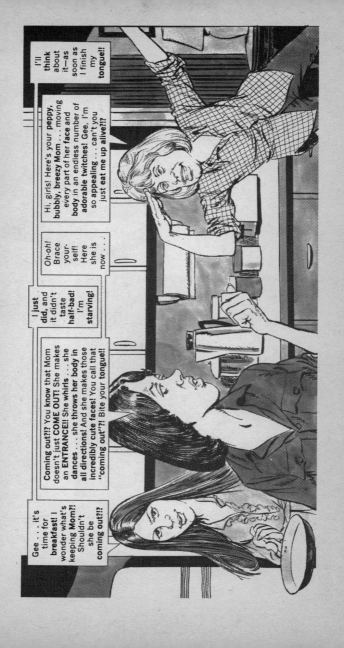

Wow! Look! She's moving parts of her face that NEVER MOVED before! Fantastic!

It's her "shtick"! All the stars on situation comedies have a shtick! Archie does "Bigot"... Maude does "Loud"... J.J. does "Cute"... and Mom does "PERKY"!

Even if this show dies, she has it made! I hear Jerry Lewis promised to raise a bundle for her on a special "Telethon" he's doing next Fall... for HEALTHY people with MUSCULAR PROBLEMS!!

Gee, Mom— isn't there any way to get you to STOP MOVING AROUND!?

A year ago, the show's Director put me into a STRAIT JACKET for a few weeks, and zipped it up over my mouth!

Where's the jacket now?

In the closet ...STILL TWITCHING!!

But enough about me! Bobka, what's your typical, relevant sitcom-type problem this week? Wait! Let me guess! You tried pot! Even better! You skipped pot and went to heroin! You can level with me! Remember, I want to help you! I love you! You mean more to me than life!
Okay! My problem is: I don't have anything to wear! None of my jeans have holes in them, and all the kids will laugh me out of school!
YOU DIRTY ROTTEN KID! YOU'RE NOT MY DAUGHTER! YOU'RE ONE OF THE BRADY BUNCH!

You call THAT a problem for a growing girl on a post-Family Hour show?!? Tonight, I'm going to lock you in the hall closet . . . and make you stay in there until you can come up with something REALLY GOOD!!
The HALL CLOSET?!? Mom, if you lock me in there with all your sick PORNO MAGAZINES, there's no telling WHAT terrible things'll happen to me!!
Well that's a START!

Girls, you've just learned a **valuable lesson! Don't ever forget it!** Namely—there is only **ONE WAY** to get **rid** of a **sex-starved letch** and have him **out** of your life **forever . . .**
And **what** way is **that,** Mom?
402
MARRY HIM!!